BUILDING BLOCKS OF PHYSICAL SCIENCE

SOUND

Written by Joseph Midthun

Illustrated by Samuel Hiti

a Scott Fetzer company
Chicago

World Book, Inc.
180 North LaSalle Street
Suite 900
Chicago, Illinois 60601
USA

For information about other World Book publications,
visit our website at **www.worldbook.com**
or call **1-800-WORLDBK (967-5325)**.
For information about sales to schools and libraries,
call 1-800-975-3250 (United States),
or 1-800-837-5365 (Canada).

Library of Congress Cataloging-in-Publication Data
for this volume has been applied for.

Building Blocks of Physical Science
ISBN: 978-0-7166-4460-6 (set, hc.)

Sound
ISBN: 978-0-7166-4470-5 (hc.)

Also available as:
ISBN: 978-0-7166-4480-4 (e-book)

1st printing March 2022

Acknowledgments:
Created by Samuel Hiti and Joseph Midthun
Art by Samuel Hiti
Additional art by David Shephard/
    The Bright Agency
Additional spot art by Dreamstime and
    Shutterstock
Text by Joseph Midthun

TABLE OF CONTENTS

What Is Sound? 4

What Makes Sound? 6

How Do We Hear Sounds? 8

Carrying Sound 10

Absorbing Sound 12

What Makes an Echo?.......................14

Sound Waves 18

How LOUD or Soft? 20

How High or Low? 22

Why Study Sound?............................28

Timeline 30

Who's Who: Griffin and Galambos.....32

Can You Believe It?!........................36

Activity: Sound Wave Model 38

Words to Know..................................39

Index 40

There is a glossary on page 39. Terms defined in the glossary are in type **that looks like this** on their first appearance.

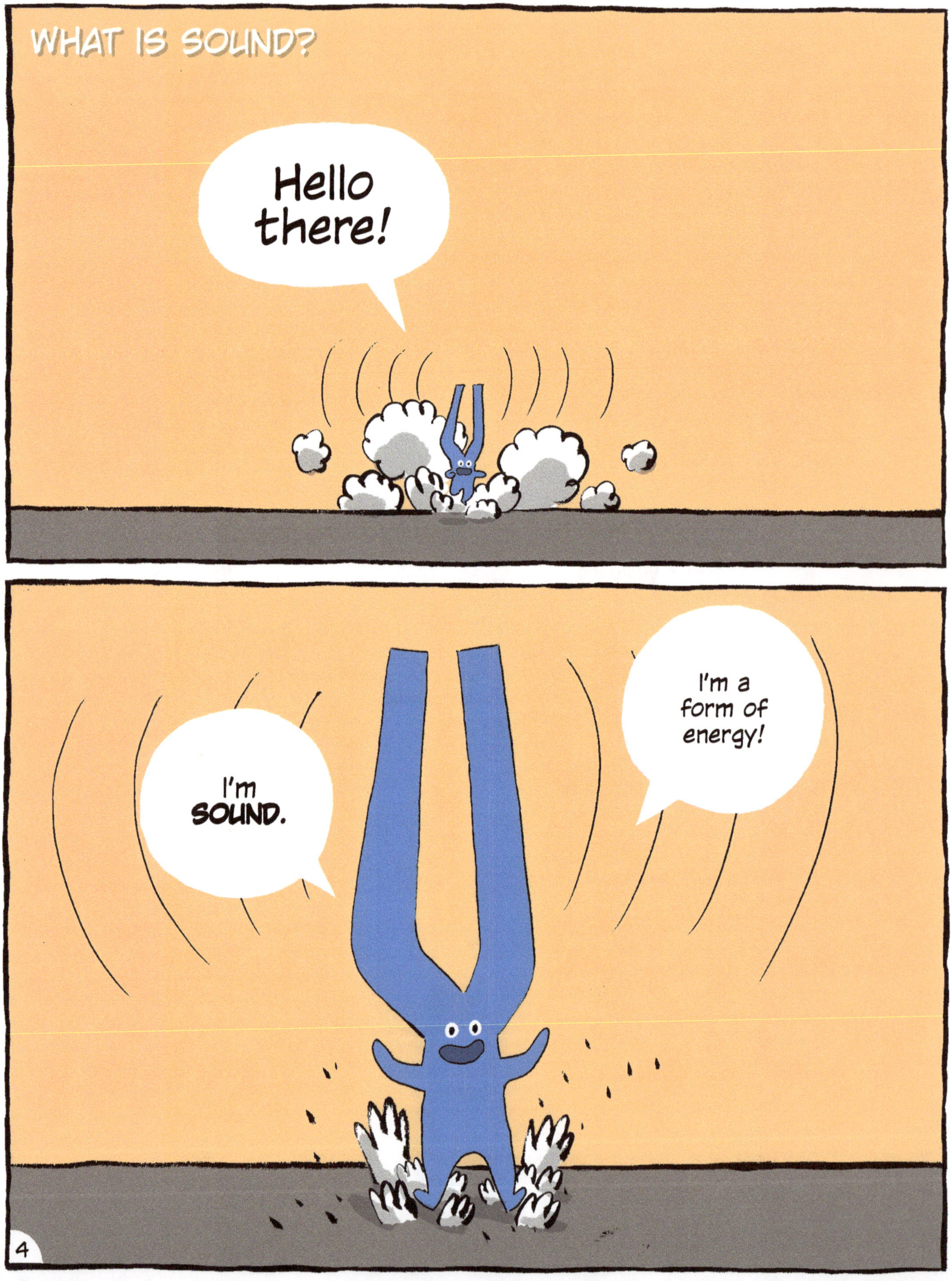

Hello there!
I'm SOUND.
I'm a form of energy!

Sound comes from objects that vibrate.
When something vibrates, it moves back and forth.

SOUNDS CAN BE LOUD!

Or sounds can be soft...

But there is more to me than meets the ear!

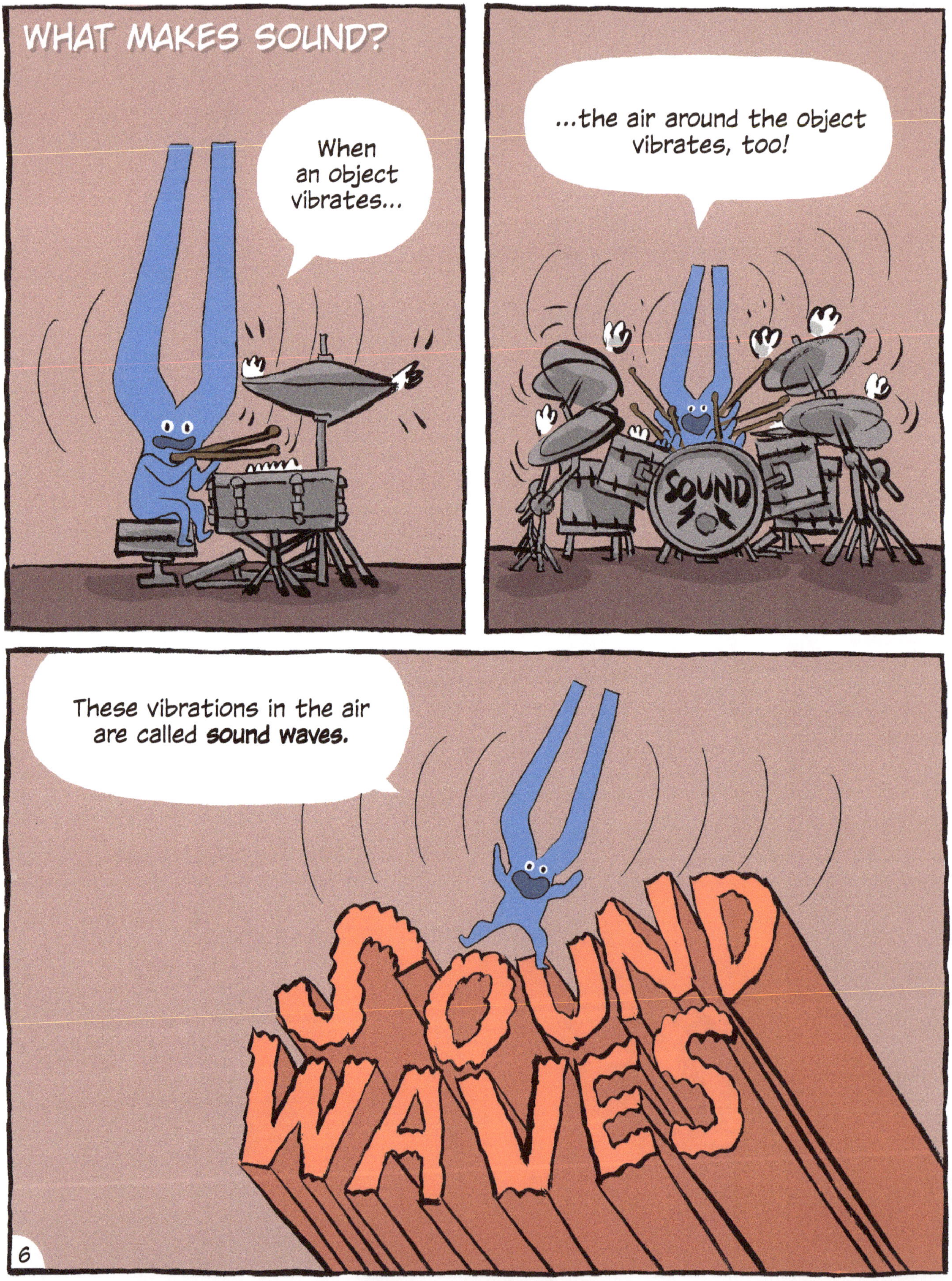

When an object vibrates...

...the air around the object vibrates, too!

These vibrations in the air are called sound waves.
SOUND WAVES

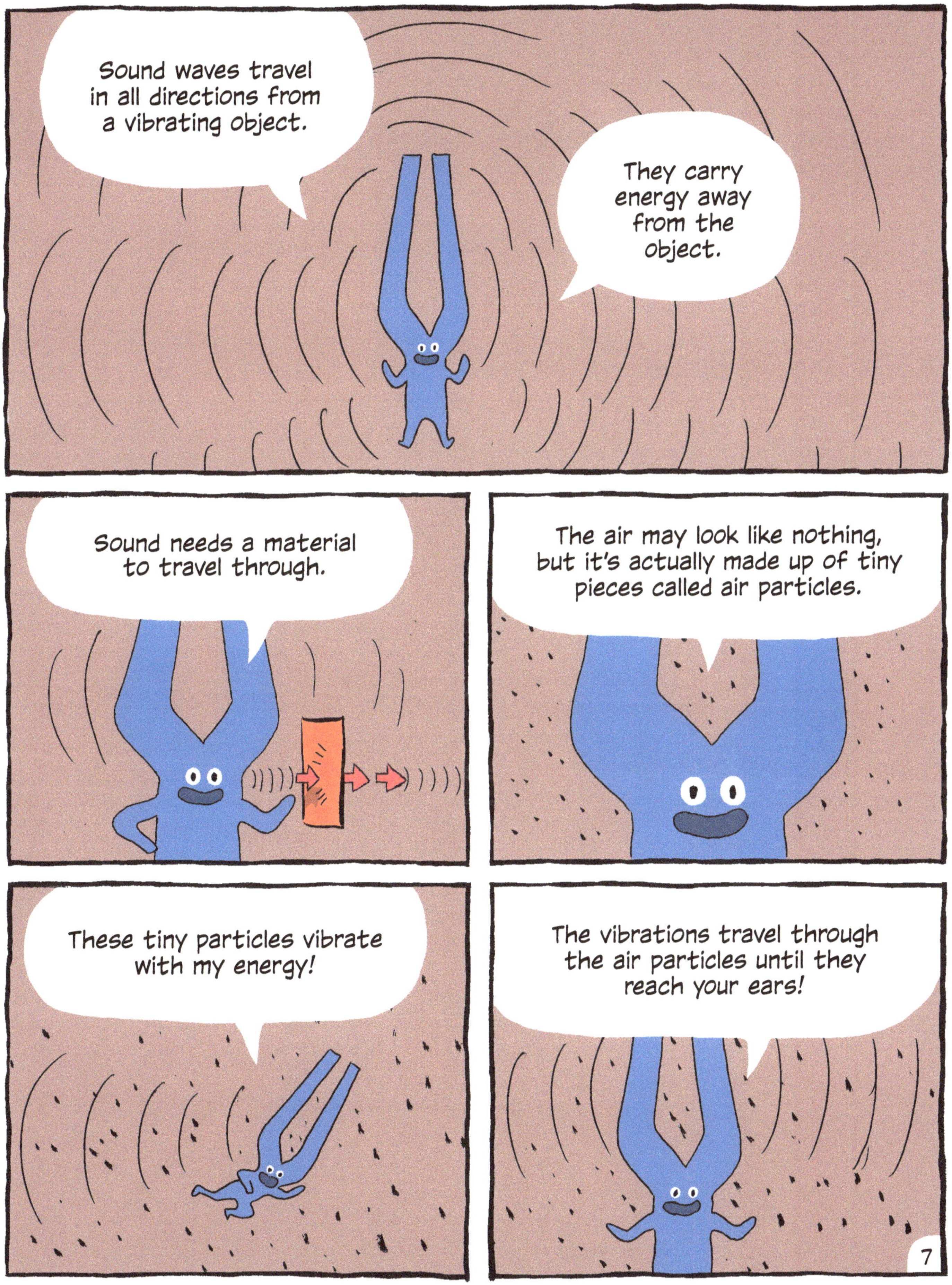

Sound waves travel in all directions from a vibrating object.
They carry energy away from the object.

Sound needs a material to travel through.

The air may look like nothing, but it's actually made up of tiny pieces called air particles.

These tiny particles vibrate with my energy!
The vibrations travel through the air particles until they reach your ears!

What happens once a sound reaches your ears?

Let's take a look inside!
ZIP

Sound waves enter your ears and hit the eardrum.
PLOP
PLOP

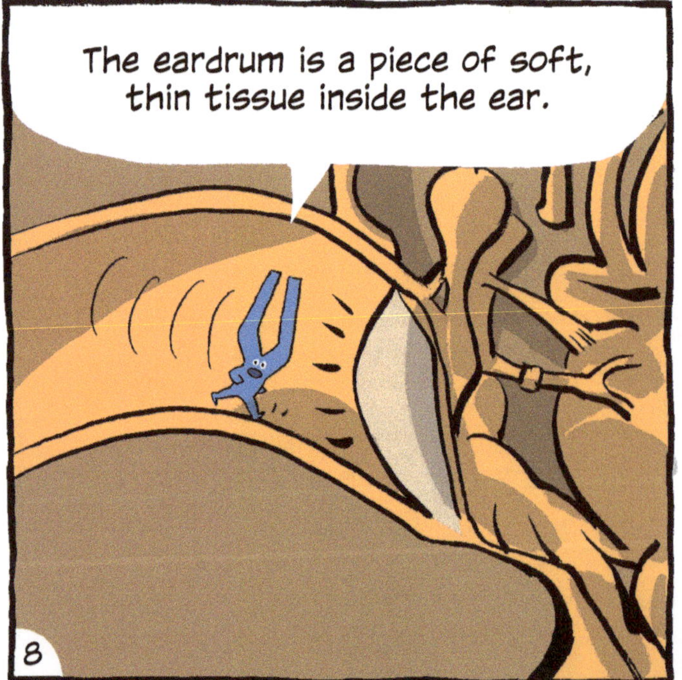
The eardrum is a piece of soft, thin tissue inside the ear.

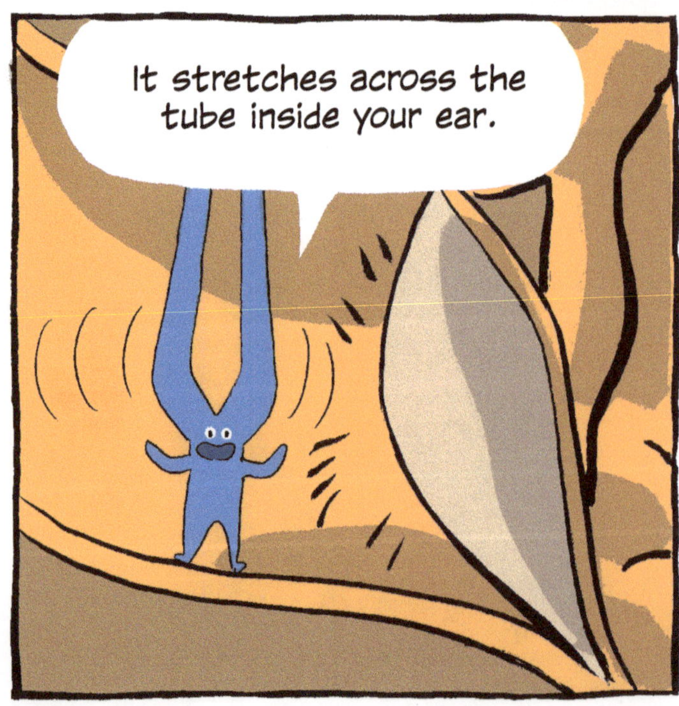
It stretches across the tube inside your ear.

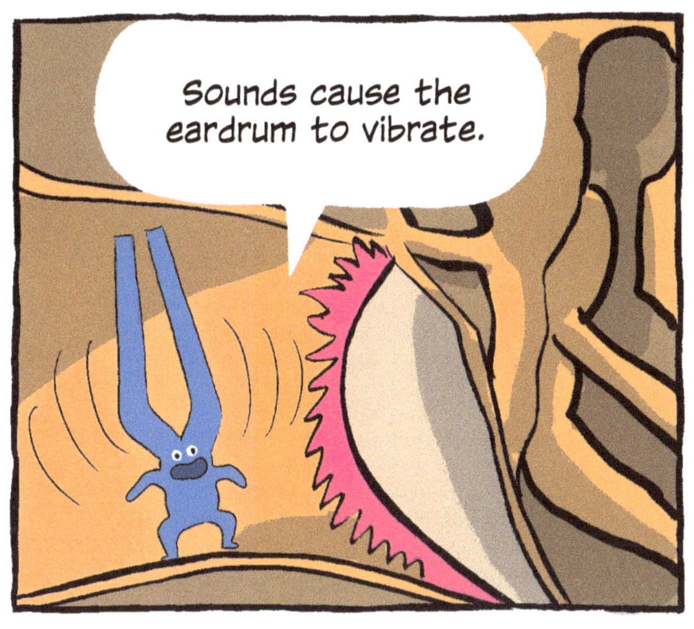
Sounds cause the eardrum to vibrate.

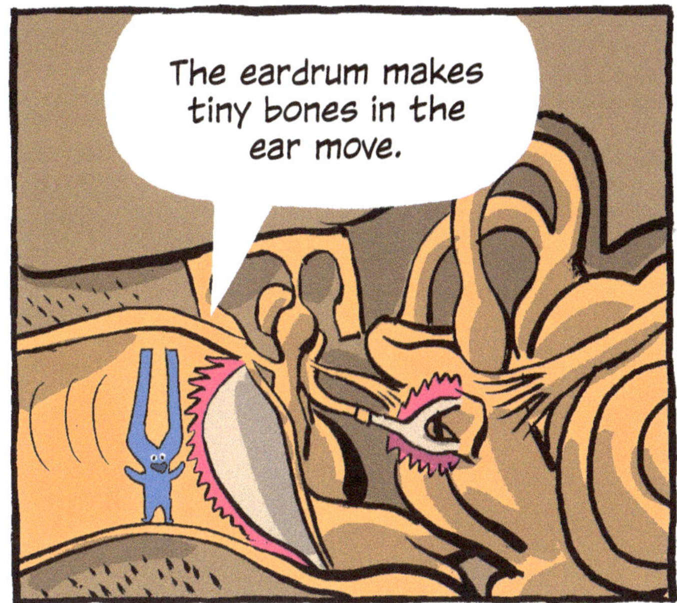
The eardrum makes tiny bones in the ear move.

These bones send the sound to a curled tube deep inside the ear called the cochlea.

The cochlea is full of liquid. As the sound waves travel through this liquid, they make tiny hairs bend.

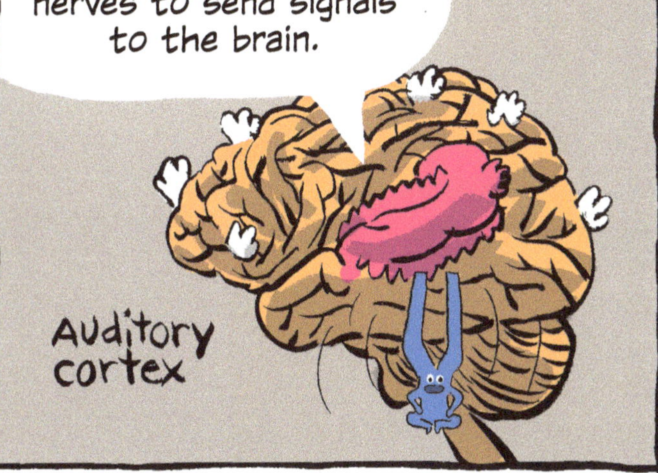
The bending hairs cause nerves to send signals to the brain.
Auditory cortex

Your brain uses these signals to perceive sound.

9

CARRYING SOUND

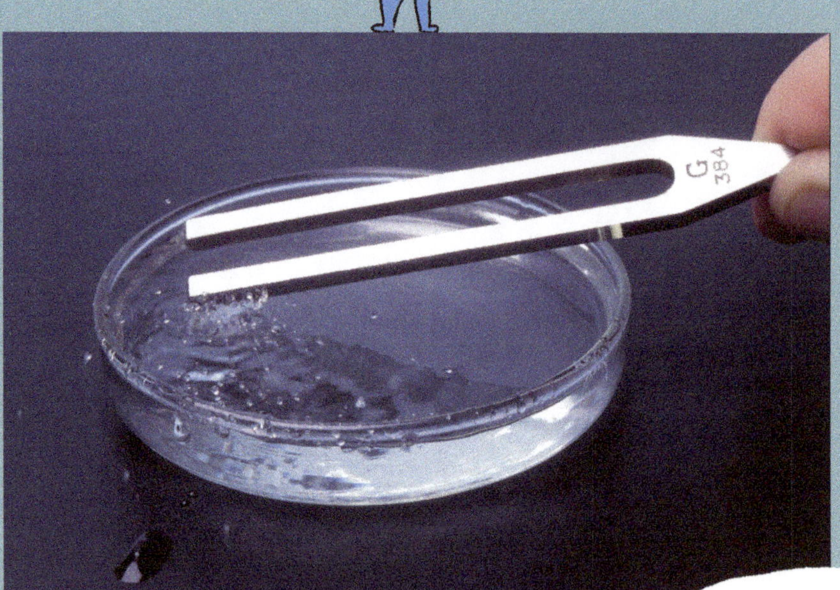

Did you know that there is no sound in outer space?
Can you guess why?
There is no air in outer space!
There are no particles to vibrate.
Without vibrations, there can be no sound.

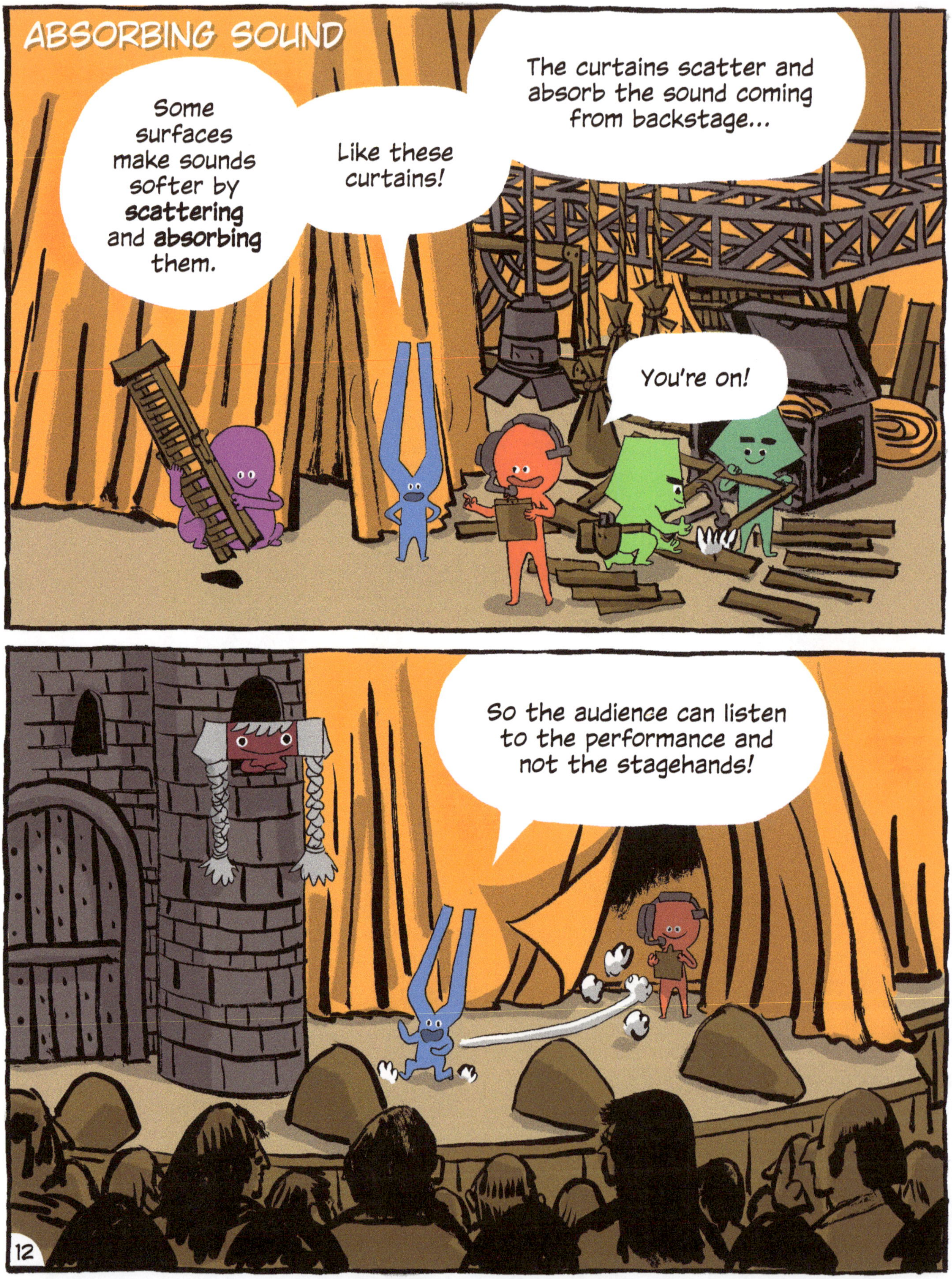

ABSORBING SOUND

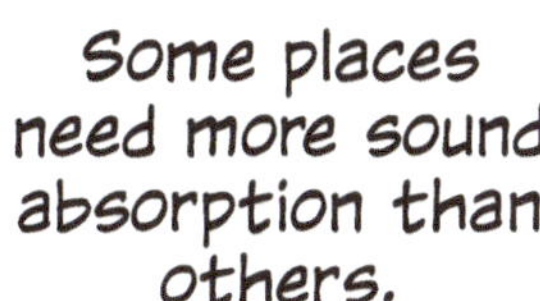

Some places need more sound absorption than others.
Recording studios, opera houses, and dance clubs are all built with sound control in mind.

TICKETS

In this concert hall, the seats are cushioned to absorb sound.
Even if the seat is empty, it absorbs as much sound as if someone were sitting there.

This way, a performance will sound the same if there are only a few people or a full house!
BRAVO!
CLAP CLAP CLAP
CLAP CLAP CLAP CLAP

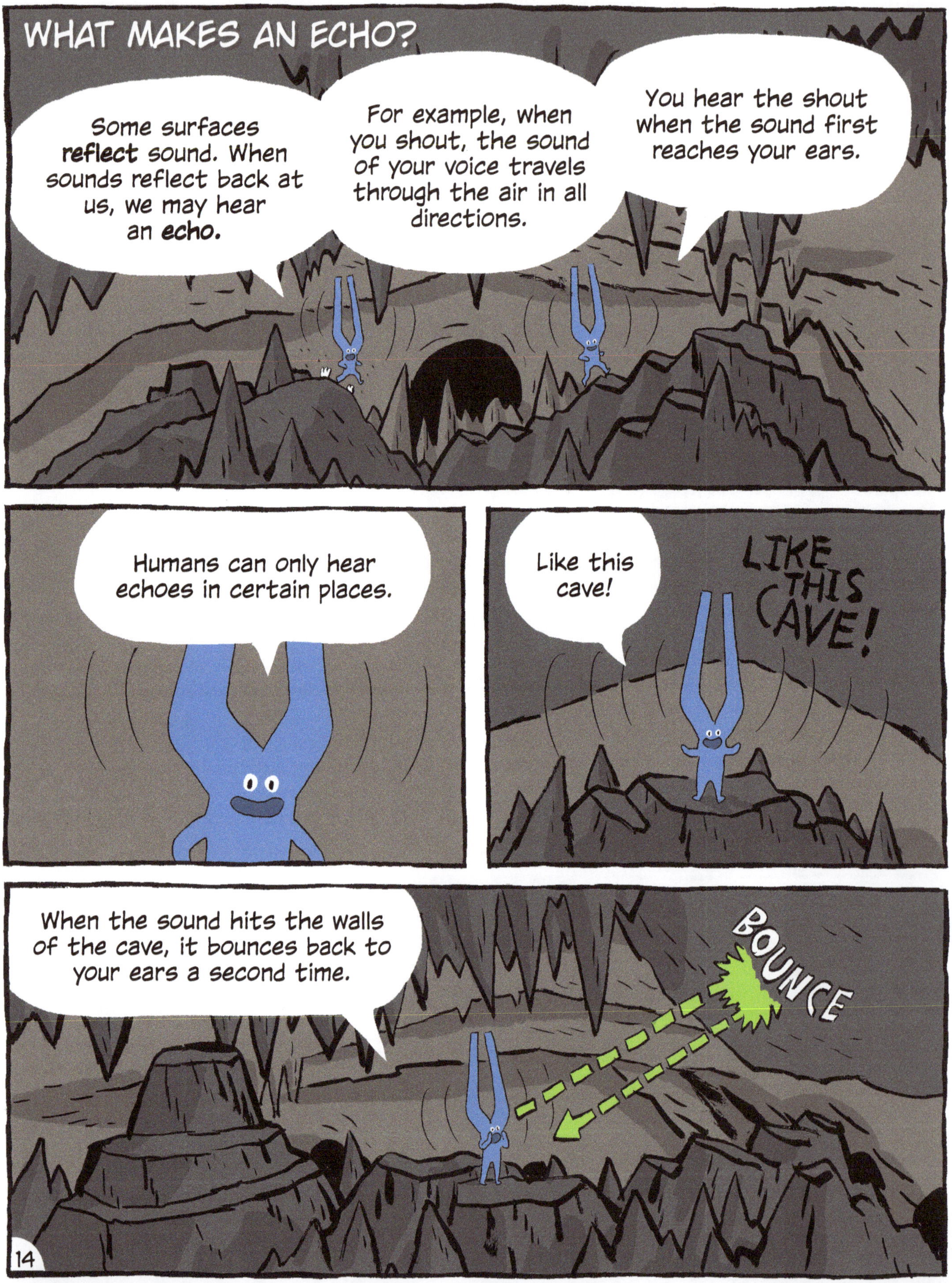

WHAT MAKES AN ECHO?

Animals with better hearing than humans hear echoes all the time!
Some animals use echoes to navigate and hunt. Bats, dolphins, and whales all use echolocation.
ECHOLOCATION
ECHOLOCATION
ECHOLOCATION
ECHOLOCATION

A bat can "see" in the dark with sound.
SWOOP
Look out!

Bats make a high-pitched sound and listen to the echoes that are reflected back.

Then the bat can measure the distance to a cave wall or even a tasty snack.

Dolphins and whales use echolocation to sense objects and other sea creatures.

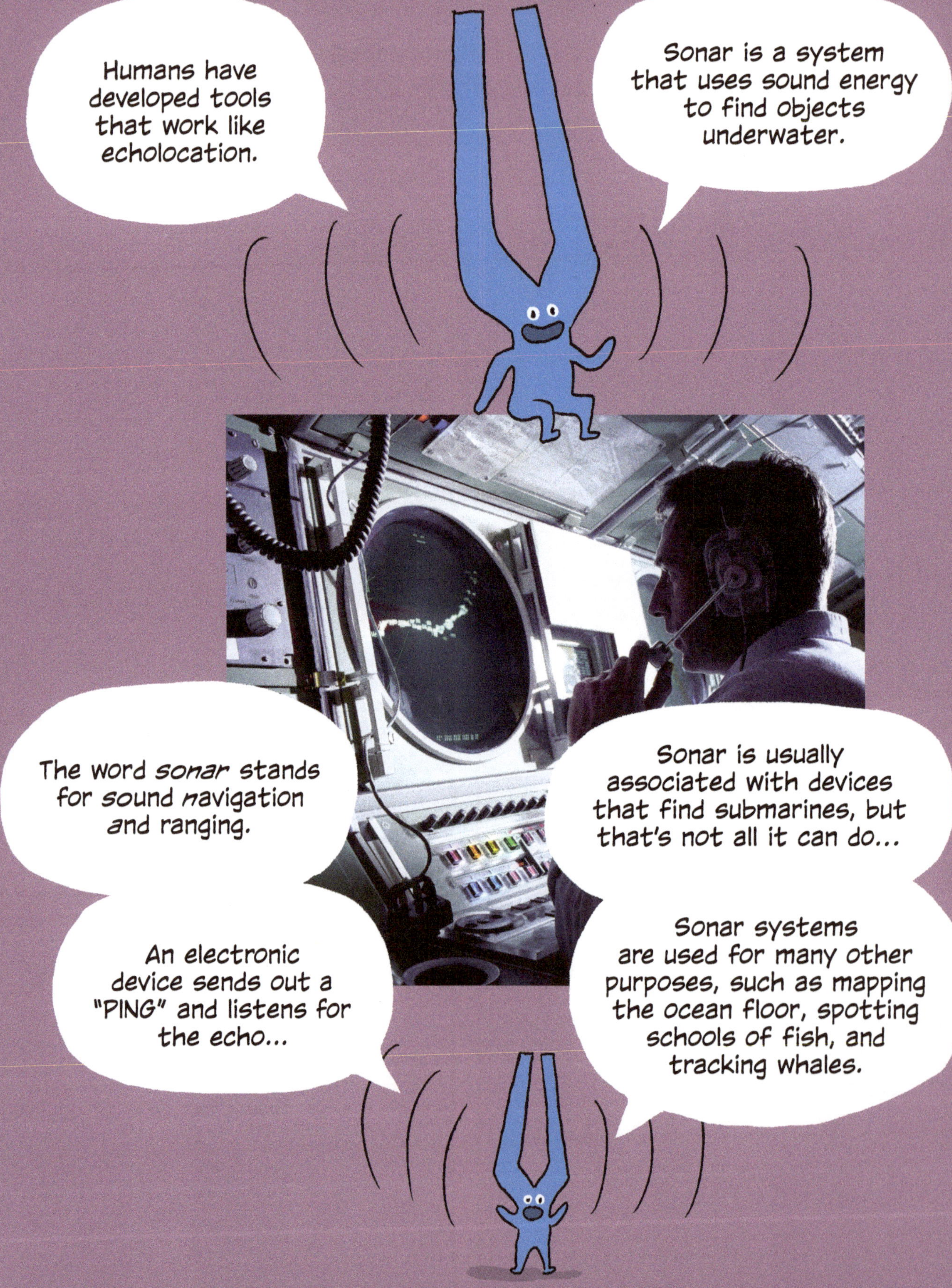

Humans have developed tools that work like echolocation.
Sonar is a system that uses sound energy to find objects underwater.
The word sonar stands for sound navigation and ranging.
Sonar is usually associated with devices that find submarines, but that's not all it can do...
An electronic device sends out a "PING" and listens for the echo...
Sonar systems are used for many other purposes, such as mapping the ocean floor, spotting schools of fish, and tracking whales.

Some burglar alarms use **ultrasound** to detect movement.

Ultrasound is a type of sonar that operates at a frequency above human hearing.

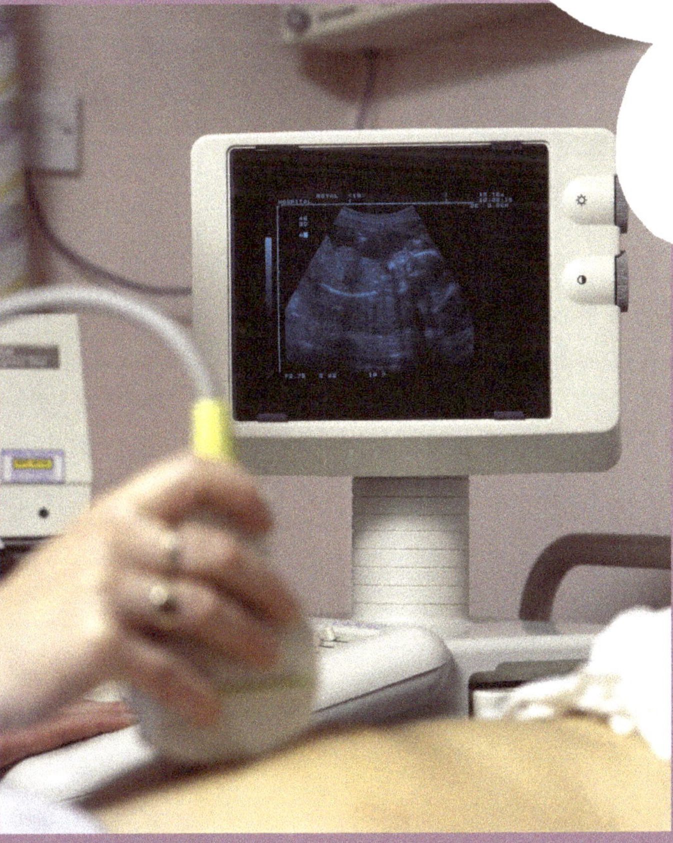

Doctors can use an ultrasound machine to take a peek inside your body!

SOUND WAVES
The shape of a sound wave can tell us about the quality of the sound.

Sound waves are somewhat like ocean waves.
They have high points and low points.

The high point of a sound wave is called a crest, or peak.

The crest represents the area of crowded particles in a sound wave.

The low point of the sound wave is called a trough, or valley.

The trough represents the area in a sound wave where the particles are farthest apart.

Sound waves are even more similar to the coils in a toy spring.

Watch what happens as this toy spring moves down the stairs.

The coils push together and spread apart.

The coils of the spring that are bunched together are the crests of the wave.

The coils that are spread apart are the troughs!

Can you think of a really loud sound?

CRASH

Loud sounds have lots of energy.

Amplitude is the amount of energy in a sound wave.

AMPLITUDE

The greater the amplitude...
...the more energy in the wave...
AMPLITUDE

THE LOUDER THE SOUND!

Some sounds you can barely hear at all...
Like a pin drop!

ping

Soft sounds have less energy than loud sounds.

HIGH
Sounds can be high...

And sounds can be low.
LOW

Have you ever wondered what makes a sound high or low?
It has to do with frequency.
FREQUENCY

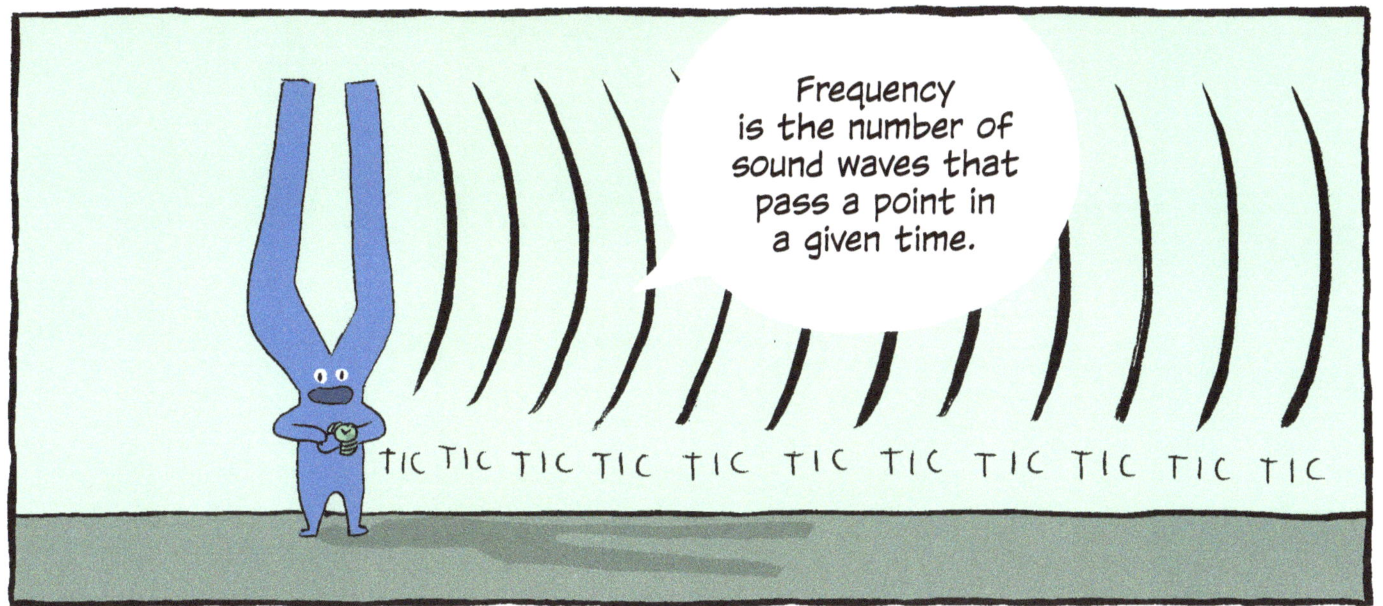

Frequency is the number of sound waves that pass a point in a given time.
TIC TIC TIC TIC TIC TIC TIC TIC TIC TIC TIC

The faster an object vibrates, the greater its frequency.

Frequency determines **pitch**—how high or low a sound is.
PITCH

High-pitched sounds have a higher frequency than low-pitched sounds.
The roar of a lion is a low-pitched sound.
ROAR.

A songbird's call is a high-pitched sound!
chirp.

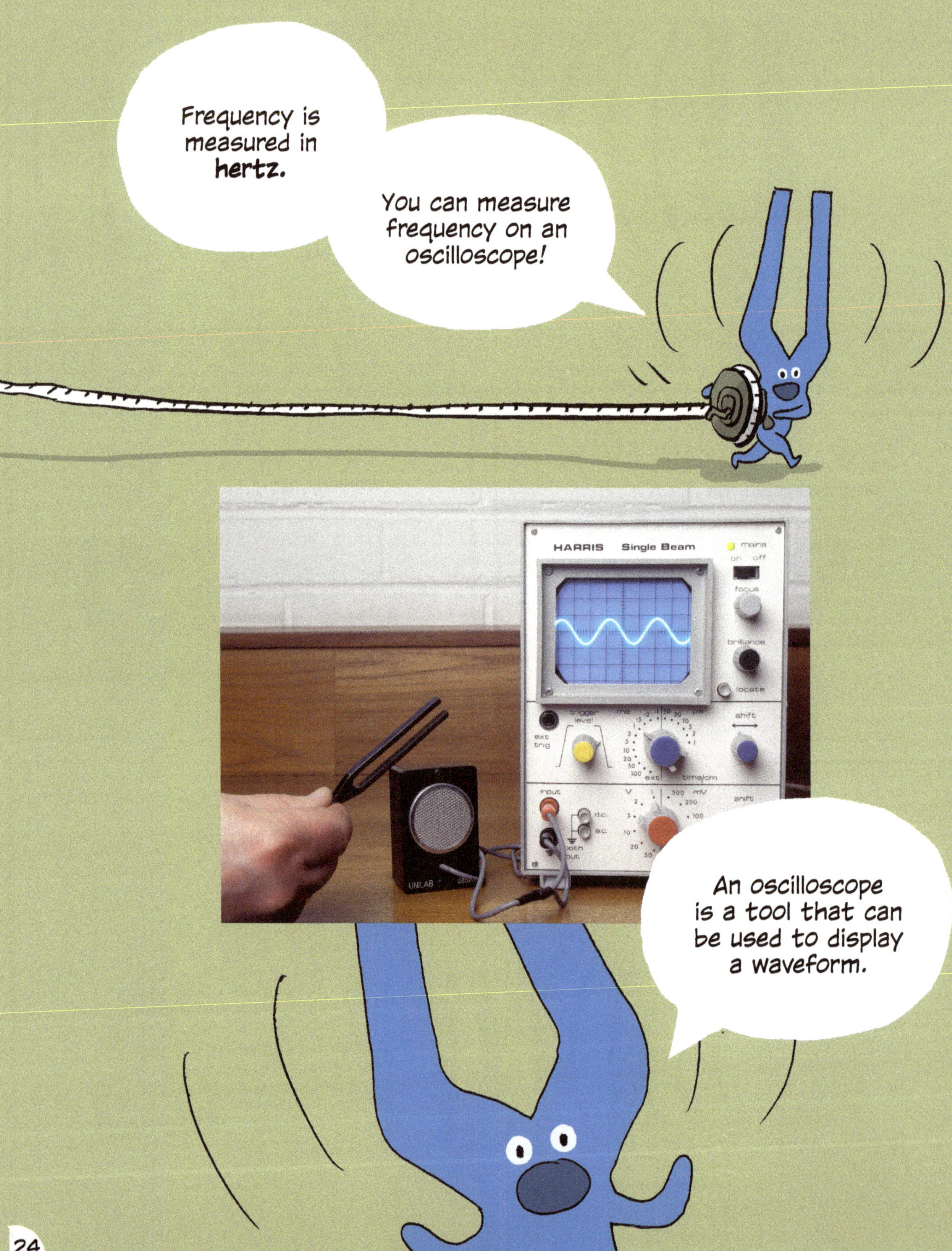

Frequency is measured in **hertz.**

You can measure frequency on an oscilloscope!

HARRIS   Single Beam

An oscilloscope is a tool that can be used to display a waveform.

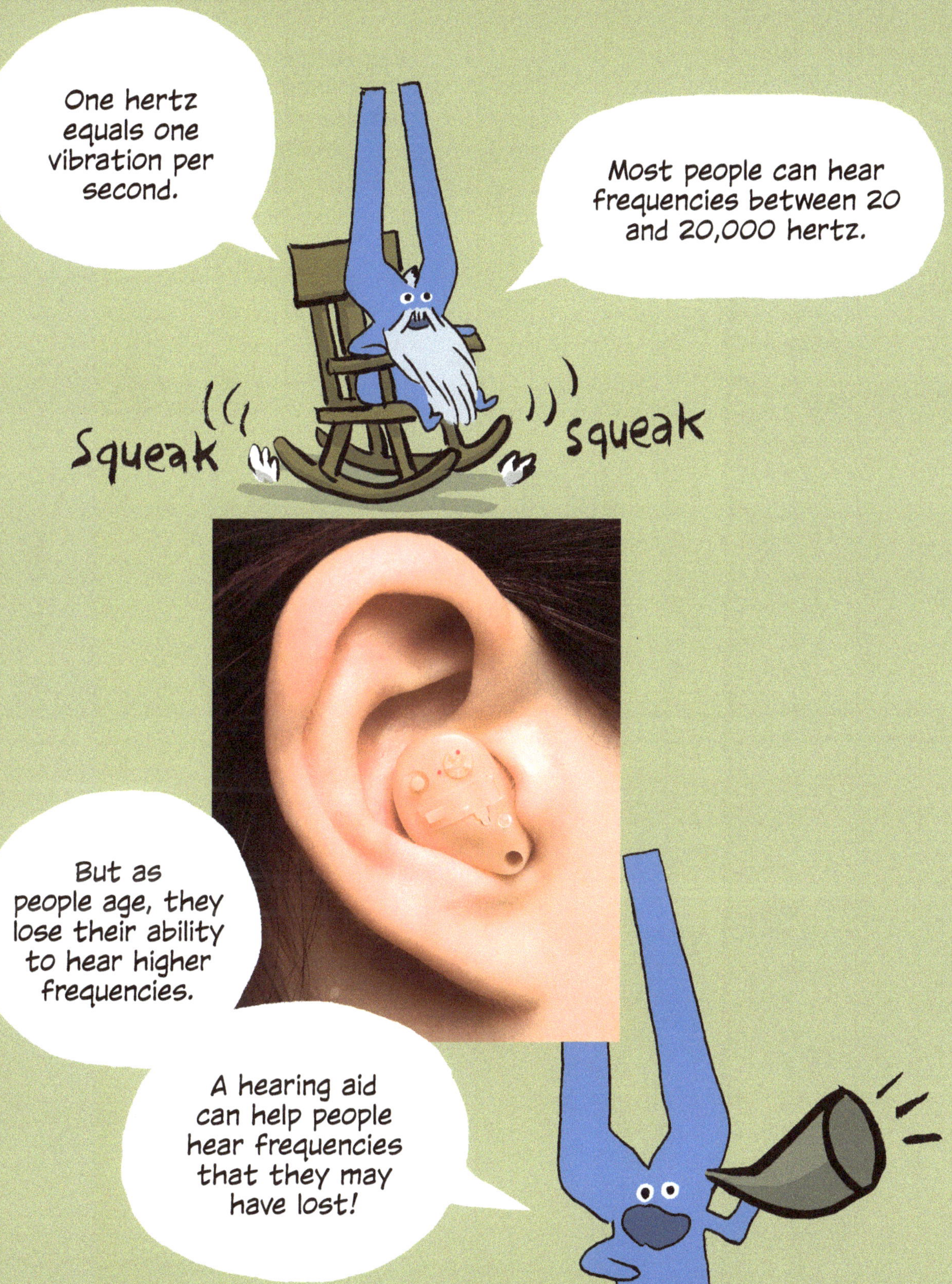

One hertz equals one vibration per second.

Most people can hear frequencies between 20 and 20,000 hertz.

Squeak

Squeak

But as people age, they lose their ability to hear higher frequencies.

A hearing aid can help people hear frequencies that they may have lost!

Many kinds of animals can hear sounds with higher or lower frequencies than a human can hear.

Elephants can coordinate their movements through low-frequency sounds and vibrations that are communicated through the ground!

This way, if they become separated, they can find each other.

This whistle makes a high-frequency sound that humans can't hear.

Dogs can, though!

Some animals can hear much softer sounds than people can.

A barn owl can hear the footsteps of its prey.

This allows the owl to hunt in complete darkness.
SWOOP

Tik
Ding Ting
Plong
Gong
Dong
People have been studying sound since ancient times.
Today, scientists use their knowledge of sound in many ways.
Ultrasound can be used to clean delicate instruments!

It can also be used to help heal wounds and injuries.

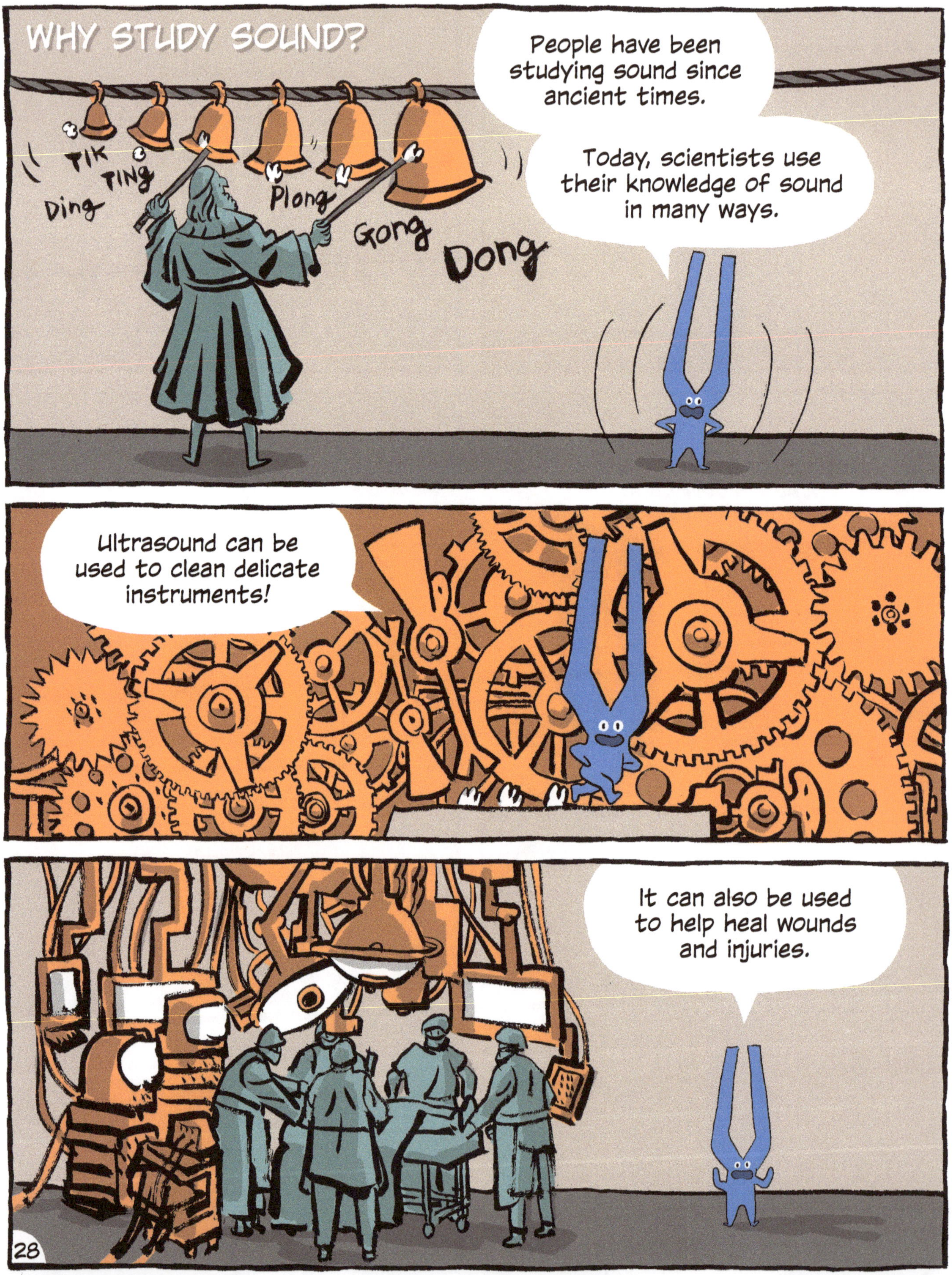

With sound, humans are able to map the floor of some of the deepest parts of the ocean!

Scientists have used sonar to discover vast underwater plains, mountain chains, and volcanoes.

And these are just a few uses of me...

Maybe you can come up with a brand-new use for me!

Hear ya 'round!

I'm SOUND!

TIMELINE

Greek
mathematician
Pythagoras
experimented
on the sounds
of vibrating
strings.

500 B.C.

Italian scientist
Leonardo da Vinci
proposed the
use of sonar in
detecting ships.

1490

1687

English scientist
Isaac Newton
published his
calculation of the
speed of sound,
but it was off by
about 20 percent.

350 B.C.

Greek philosopher
Aristotle suggested
that the movement
of air carries sound
to our ears.

1638

Italian
scientist Galileo
demonstrated that
the frequency
of sound waves
determines their
pitch.

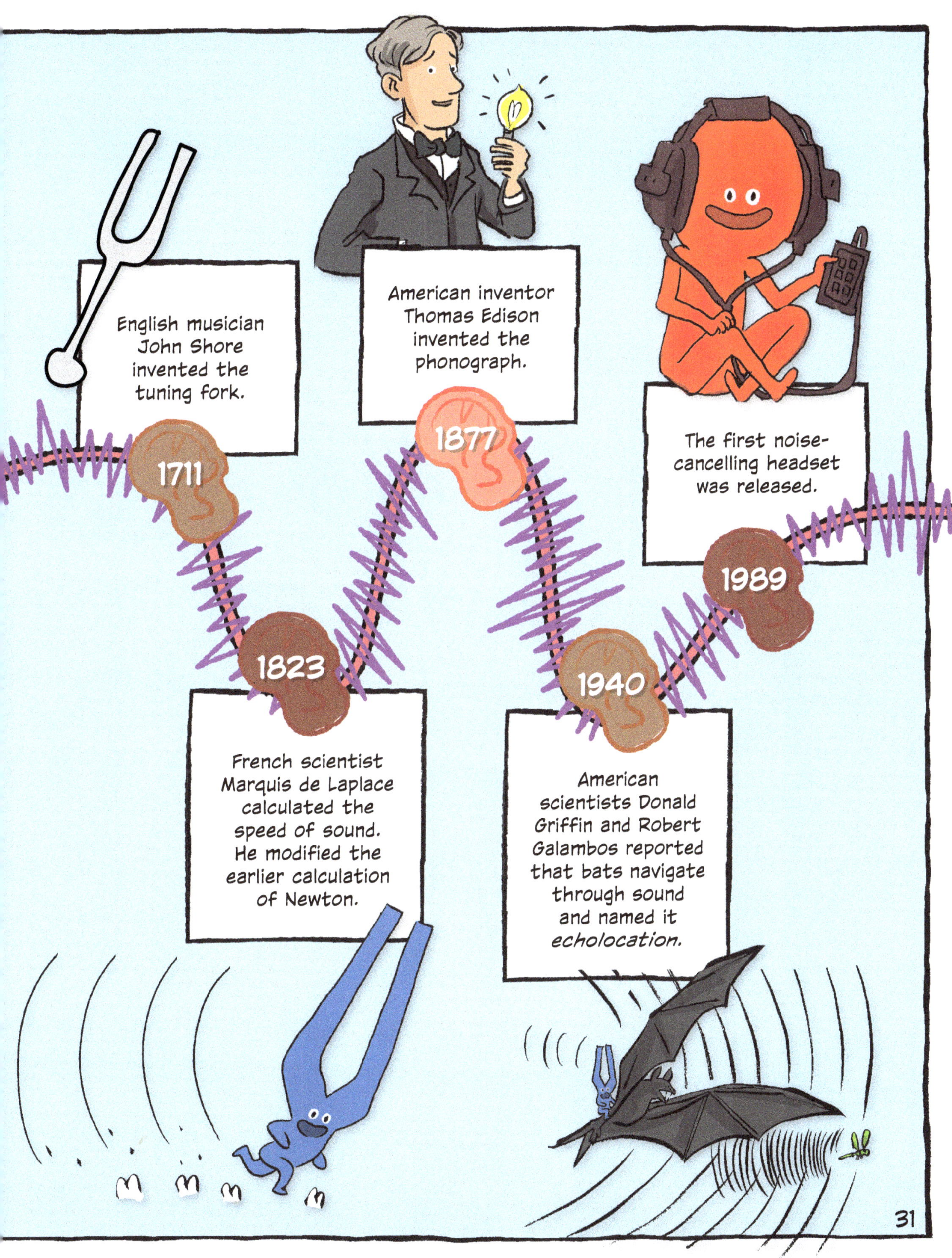

English musician John Shore invented the tuning fork.
1711
American inventor Thomas Edison invented the phonograph.
1877
The first noise-cancelling headset was released.
1989
French scientist Marquis de Laplace calculated the speed of sound. He modified the earlier calculation of Newton.
1823
American scientists Donald Griffin and Robert Galambos reported that bats navigate through sound and named it echolocation.
1940

WHO'S WHO:
GRIFFIN AND
GALAMBOS

Perfect! The bat was able to navigate around you!
Why is there a bat on my head? And who are you guys?

I'm Donald Griffin. I discovered that bats can make high-frequency sounds that humans can't hear.

And I'm Robert Galambos. I discovered that they can hear these and other high-frequency sounds.

Together, we're trying to show that they use those abilities to navigate.

In our lab, we've used wires to create a maze for bats. We release one bat and see how it flies.
Then we plug its ears or tie its mouth shut—
-and release it again.
These impairments are easily reversible!

Fact File

Name: Donald Griffin

Born: 1915 in Southampton, New York, USA

Occupation: Scientist

Claim to fame: Proved echolocation in bats, studied animal cognition.

Fact File

Name: Robert Galambos

Born: 1914 in Lorain, Ohio, USA

Occupation: Scientist

Claim to fame: Proved echolocation in bats, studied how the brain processes sound.

Some jet airplanes **travel faster** than the speed of sound! They create loud sonic booms when they do.

A passenger jet called the **Concorde** made supersonic flights across the Atlantic Ocean, but it was retired in 2003.

Scientists use a unit called the *decibel* (dB) to measure sound intensity. Breathing is about 10 decibels. A normal spoken conversation is about 50 decibels.

A jet airplane takeoff

is about 150!

The speed of sound

through air is 1,116 feet (340 meters) per second.

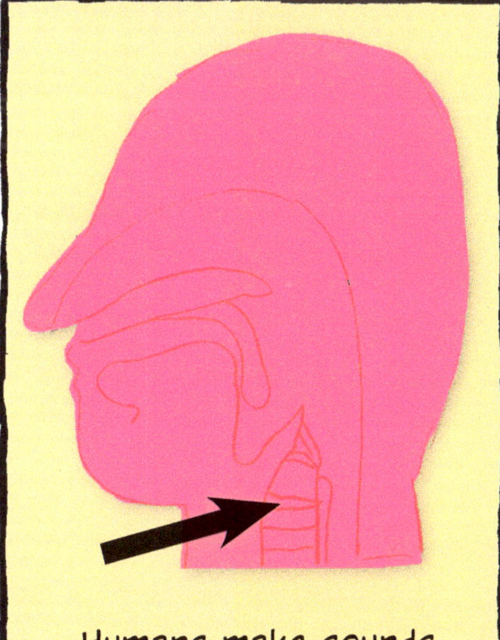

Humans make sounds in a part of the throat called

the larynx.

The **Doppler effect** is the change in frequency of sound caused by the relative motion of the source of the waves. It makes trains sound higher pitched as they

move toward you.

ACTIVITY:
SOUND WAVE MODEL

Sound waves travel through air to our ears. The particles of air vibrate backward and forward but do not travel with sound. This model will show you how sound waves travel.

Step 1: Cut six pieces of string, each 10 inches (25 centimeters) long, and attach one end of each string to a glass marble using tape.

Step 2: Tie the other end of each string to the horizontal piece of a clothes hanger, leaving about 1 inch (2.5 centimeters) between each thread that you tie.

Step 3: Hang the hook of the clothes hanger. Pull back one of the end marbles. Let the marble go so that it strikes the next marble. Watch what happens.

Step 4: Each marble hits the next marble, which swings to the side and hits the next marble, and so on. But the marbles themselves do not change position on the hanger.

Step 5: Sound travels through the air in the same way.

A vibration causes one molecule of air to move from side to side and bump into another molecule, which then moves from side to side at the same rate and bumps into a third molecule, and so on.

What You'll Need
- String
- Scissors
- Ruler
- Six glass marbles or beads
- Tape
- Clothes hanger

WORDS TO KNOW

absorb to take in and hold rather than reflect.

amplitude the amount of energy in a wave.

cochlea a spiral-shaped cavity of the inner ear.

crest the highest point of a sound wave. The crest represents the area where particles in the wave are crowded together.

distance the amount of space between two points.

eardrum the part of the ear that vibrates in response to sounds.

echo a reflected sound.

echolocation the use of sound by certain animals to sense their surroundings. Bats and dolphins use echolocation.

frequency the number of sound waves or light waves that pass by one point in a given time.

hertz a unit used to measure sound frequency. One hertz equals one cycle (sound wave) per second.

pitch the highness or lowness of a sound.

reflect to throw back light, heat, sound, or other form of energy. Reflection occurs when energy or an object bounces off a surface.

scatter to separate and drive off in different directions.

sound wave energy that moves through a material, such as air or water, as a vibration.

states of matter the different forms of matter. The most familiar are solid, liquid, and gas.

trough the lowest point of a sound wave. The trough represents the area where particles in the wave are spread farthest apart.

ultrasound sound that is too high-pitched for human beings to hear.

INDEX

absorption, 12-13
air, 6-7, 10
amplitude, 20-21
animals, 15, 23, 26-27
auditory cortex, 9

bats, 15
brain, 9
burglar alarms, 17

cochlea, 9
crests, 18-19

dogs, 27
dolphins, 15

eardrum, 8-9
ears, 8-9
echo, 14-17
echolocation, 15, 16, 32-35
elephants, 26
energy, 4, 7, 20-21

frequency, 22-23
    hearing of, 25-27
    measuring, 24-25

gases, 10

hearing, 8-9, 24-27
hearing aids, 25
hertz, 24-25

liquids, 10

matter, 10

ocean mapping, 16, 29
oscilloscopes, 24
owls, 27

pitch, 22-23

scattering, 12
solids, 10
sonar, 16, 29
sound, 4-5
    absorbing, 12-13
    causes of, 6-7
    echoing of, 14-17
    hearing, 8-9, 25-27
    loudness of, 5, 20-21
    pitch of, 22-23
    reasons for studying, 28-29
    travel by, 7, 10-11
sound waves, 6-7
    amplitude of, 20-21
    frequency of, 22-27
    in ear, 8-9
    shapes of, 18-19
space, 11

troughs, 18-19

ultrasound, 17, 28

vibrations, 5-7
    frequency and, 23
    of eardrum, 9
    space and, 11

waves. *See* sound waves
whales, 15